D0116365

T2-AKH-148

Brazil

Brazil is the fifth largest country in the world with a large and rapidly growing population. It is a country of contrasts. Geographically, Brazil has a wide variety of different landscapes: the tropical jungle of the Amazon region; the dry and flat areas of the interior; and the long stretches of magnificent coastline. Racially, Brazil is a blend of native Indian, European, and African. Socially, a wide gulf exists between the rich and the poor. The present government is trying to combat this problem by harnessing Brazil's material and human resources in a program of economic development. Brazil's economy is still reliant on agricultural exports, but industries, like ship building and car production, are playing an increasingly important part.

In *We live in Brazil*, a cross section of the Brazilian people, young and old, men and women, tell you what life is like in their home country – life in the big cities, in tiny villages, in the countryside, and along the banks of the mighty Amazon. The author, Patricia Robb, is a journalist who has lived and worked in Brazil for many years.

we live in
BRAZIL

Patricia Robb

The Bookwright Press
New York · 1985

Living Here

First published in the United States in 1985 by
The Bookwright Press, 387 Park Avenue South,
New York, NY 10016
First published in 1984 by
Wayland (Publishers) Ltd
49 Lansdowne Place, Hove
East Sussex BN3 1HF, England

ISBN: 0–531–03821–1

Library of Congress Catalog Card Number: 84–72047
Printed in Italy by G. Canale & C.S.p.A., Turin

Contents

"When we play the fans go wild"

Brazil is one of the world's supreme soccer nations and frequent winner of the World Cup. João Batista Nunes de Oliveira, known as "Nunes," is a center forward with the Clube de Regatas do Flamengo, the most popular soccer club in Brazil with an outstanding record of wins.

In Brazil, we begin kicking a soccer ball almost as soon as we learn how to walk. By the time I was eight years old, I had already developed the knack and was playing in the boys' team of the local club in Ferra de Santana, in the state of Bahia, where I was born. When I was twelve, a soccer coach from Rio's Flamengo Club was up in Bahia. He visited the club and saw me play. Soon afterward I was invited to come to Rio and train with the Flamengo Youth Group. It was a marvelous opportunity because Rio is the center of soccer in Brazil. Flamengo is the hottest soccer club in Brazil and turns out some of the country's best players.

I turned professional while still a teenager, and played for a team in the northern state of Sergipe. Later, I played with a team in Recife called Santa Cruz. In 1978, I was chosen to play in the Brazilian team in the World Cup Games held in Argentina. I spent one year playing with the Monte Rei Team in Mexico and six months playing with a team in Houston, Texas, in the United States. When I returned to Brazil in 1980, I joined Flamengo and have been with them ever since.

At the Flamengo Soccer Club in Rio, Nunes shows some boys a few soccer tricks.

Brazilians are the best fans any soccer players could want. When we play at the Maracanã Stadium in Rio, which is one of the world's largest and holds up to 200,000 spectators, the fans go wild. They wave huge red-and-black flags, the colors of Flamengo, and throw firecrackers and talcum bombs. The Maracanã Stadium was built in 1950 to accommodate the World Cup Games. Due to the explosive nature of the Brazilian fans, it was designed with a 2.7-meter (9-foot) deep moat around it to keep the excited spectators off the field.

Although the English invented soccer and introduced it to Brazil in 1906, the Brazilians have made the sport their own. When a Brazilian player gets hold of the ball, he does some wonderfully artistic and skillful things with it. He creates a special relationship between the man and the ball. Besides being a game of speed, Brazilians consider it a contest of concentration and technique, which is the difference between Brazilian soccer and that of other countries.

Soccer plays an important part in the lives of Brazilians. It makes up a major part of the news. Our faces are known by the people and we become public idols. Every Brazilian boy at some time or another has dreamt of being a *craque* (a soccer star). I was lucky because the dream came true for me. But because of the fame that comes with it, I can't always lead a normal life. I love the beach, but I don't go often because people recognize me and come running over. So I usually spend my free time with my wife and our two-year-old daughter at the private clubs. Also, I enjoy discotheques, but have to limit the time I spend there because an athlete needs plenty of sleep too.

The goaltender makes a brave save during an exciting match at the huge Maracanã Stadium.

"I love the quietness and peace"

Pedro Paulo Carneiro Lopes, or "Pepe," is a hang-gliding champion. He lives in Rio de Janeiro, the international capital for hang-gliding pilots, where he can practice the exciting sport every day.

When I am hang-gliding, I feel completely free, like a bird flying in the sky. I love the quietness and peace of being up there and looking around and seeing nothing but air. It's just me and the sky. Rio de Janeiro's beautiful mountains and beaches are among the best in the world for hang-gliding pilots. One of my favorite launching sites is Pedra Bonita, a peak in the Gávea Mountains that is 600 meters (1,980 feet) high. Jumping from there, I land on a stretch of beach called São Conrado, one of the many beaches on Brazil's 7,336-kilometer (4,400-mile) long Atlantic coastline. Large weekend crowds always gather on the beach to watch us soar through the air. Besides local beach-goers, there are lots of tourists from Europe, other South American countries and the U.S. who are enthusiastic about the sport.

From Rio, going south about 154 kilometers (93 miles) to an area called Angra dos Reis, the shoreline is so lush and green that they call it the "Green Coast." It's a real paradise with mountains, rich vegetation, unspoiled beaches and over 300 islands. Among the tropical foliage you can see palm trees and banana plants.

There are many *Cariocas* (natives of Rio)

Flying above the Brazilian flag, Pepe shows off his skills to the watching crowd.

like me who love to spend the whole day at the beach. Sometimes we skip lunch or munch snacks sold by vendors who roam the beaches. The suntanned peddlers with their large silver tanks full of lemonade and *matte*, a typical Brazilian tea heavily laced with sugar, do a busy trade. Since I use up a lot of energy on the beach, I know how important it is to eat properly. Because of this, I opened a health food lunch stall on the Pepino Beach near the landing site for hang-gliders. There I sell freshly-squeezed fruit juices, of which Brazil has plenty, along with such items as sandwiches made from wholewheat bread and natural cheeses. It was such a success that I opened another stall in the neighboring beach, Barra da Tijuca.

I think that Brazilians are now more aware than ever before of their bodies and health. We are learning the importance of physical fitness and a good diet. We appreciate the natural beauty and warm climate of Rio and take advantage of it by becoming some of the world's best surfers and hang-gliders.

Pepe about to land his hang-glider on Pepino Beach in São Conrado, Rio.

"There are about 720,000 Indians in Brazil"

Messias is an Indian boy who lives on Terra Nova Island near the junction of the Negro and Solimões rivers which combine to form the mighty Amazon. Like his ancestors, he makes Indian crafts which he sells to island visitors.

I was born here on Terra Nova Island. I live in the village with my family. We have a simple wooden house. I go to elementary school on the island, but when I am older I'll have to go by boat to a school in the city of Manaus. The island school is only for young children.

When people come to visit the island, my mother and I take the Indian crafts we make down to the docks. We wait for the boats to come in, and display our

A craftshop in Manaus displays feathered body ornaments made by local Indians.

necklaces and bows and arrows on the path, so everybody can see them when they pass by. My mother taught me how to make the necklaces. We gather all kinds of seeds and beans and let them dry. Some are white, others speckled; some are round, others oval. We string them together and sometimes we use feathers and shells that we find on the island to decorate the necklaces. We make bows and arrows that look like the ones which the Amazon Indians use for hunting. My mother carves the wood for them and I string fish bones and seeds to tie on the arrows. They're more difficult to make than the necklaces.

We also make *maracas* out of dried gourds. The Indians who still live in tribes in the interior use *maracas* as musical instruments during their rituals. We decorate the gourds with strings and seeds and feathers or carve an Indian face on them.

Some Brazilian Indians still live in tribes. But they're in remote places that are difficult to get to. My teacher said there are about 720,000 Indians in Brazil, the majority of them living in the Amazon region. Near Terra Nova Island live the Tukanos, Tieutinas, Barés and Awarates Indians. They too make crafts but they rarely leave their Indian reservations in the jungle. Once in a while, one or two will come to deliver the feather arrangements and baskets which they have made. The government has a store in Manaus where the crafts are sold. There are bracelets, headdresses, armlets and earrings made of palm fiber and feathers.

I like living on the island and selling Indian crafts to visitors. Lots of people come to Terra Nova to see the *Encontro das Aguas*, the meeting of the two rivers that form the Amazon. One is very dark and called the Negro River, and the other has light-brown muddy water and is called the Solimões River. When the two meet, the strangest thing happens — they don't mix. You can see a line; on one side the water is dark and on the other it is light. The island is near the meeting of the waters, so people stop here on their way and look at the cacao trees, manioc plantations and rubber trees.

Messias and his friend Valdo prepare their crafts to sell to visitors to the island.

11

"The Amazon is the largest river in the world"

João Barros Feitosa works at the port of Manaus which is on the Negro River, a tributary of the Amazon River. Since the age of 16 he has loaded the boats of traders who come from the lake regions of the Amazon River and its 1,100 tributaries.

They say the Amazon jungle is one of the world's greatest natural wonders, and that parts of it are still unknown to man. The area that I know best is the Amazon River itself and its main tributary, the Negro River. The Amazon is the largest river in the world, some 6,540 kilometers (4,087 miles) long. Some 3,594 kilometers (2,246 miles) of it pass through Brazilian territory.

I live in Manaus, the commercial center of the Amazon area, which is located on the Negro River at the point where its waters are 16 kilometers (10 miles) wide. It is called the Negro River because its

Traders arrive at Manaus from the lake regions of the Amazon to sell and buy goods.

waters are darkened by silt from the Andes Mountains where the river rises.

The rivers are very important to us. Many big ships travel between the city of Belem, near the mouth of the Amazon River where the waters meet the Atlantic Ocean, and Manaus, bringing their goods to trade.

We also trade with the inland region of the Amazon basin. Our fresh fruit and vegetables come from the remote towns of Santa Rein and Tabatinga via the waterways. Regional fish such as tambaqui, tucunaré and pirarucu, the largest river fish in the world, are delivered to the port by local fishermen.

The traders from the interior are called *regatões*. They are wandering river peddlers who come to Manaus to buy and sell. They trade their bananas for coffee or other goods that come all the way from the southern industrial states. Working at the dock, I unload their produce and fill their empty boats with sacks of corn, beans and rice as well as boxes of cigarettes, soap, beer and other things the river folk might need.

Loading the boats is hard and heavy work. The sacks weigh about 50 kg (110 lb) each. The day is long and hot. I arrive at the dock at 7 a.m. and leave at 6 p.m. I don't work constantly, only when the boats arrive, but with temperatures averaging 35°C (95°F) one really works up a sweat. To cool off, we drink plenty of beer. Between loads, we play pool or cards to pass the time while we wait for the next boat to arrive. On weekends, I swim and play soccer on a beach close by called Ponta Negra.

I was born in Cruzeiro do Sul, the capital of the small state of Acre, which lies southwest from Amazonas, Brazil's largest state. When I was a boy, my parents decided to move to Manaus because it's the main gateway to the Amazon region and offers more opportunities. The city began to prosper in the late nineteenth century due to the developing rubber industry. Public buildings, bridges and even an opera house were constructed, only a stone's throw away from the jungle.

Manaus is still an important town, even today. It lies in Brazil's northern region which covers an area of 3,577,000 square kilometers (1,380,722 square miles) and makes up 60 percent of the country. The region has the lowest population density in Brazil, averaging only one inhabitant per square kilometer. But things are changing now: they are cutting down the jungle and resettling people from the overcrowded cities in the south. It sounds like a good idea, but the experiment is causing a lot of unhappiness among the people who have been resettled here. I like living close to the river, but it does not suit everyone.

While waiting for the boats to arrive, João watches the barmaid play with her pet snake.

13

"Manaus was the rubber capital of the world"

Jandira Cordovil Nascimento and her family live in the Guamá Agro industrial farming complex in Belem, in the state of Para. She works as a rubber tapper for Pirelli, the firm that owns and cultivates the farm's 800 hectares (2,000 acres) of *seringueiras* (rubber trees).

Have you ever wondered where rubber comes from? Well, it comes from trees which we call *seringueiras*. My husband and I are both *seringueiros*, or rubber tappers. Our job is to cut the tree at the right angle to extract the most milk, or latex. We learned our job here at the Guamá farm where we trained for one week to learn the cutting technique. If you can't get the hang of it in the one week training period, you'll never be a rubber tapper.

My day begins at 5:30 a.m. when I go out to the plantation and start cutting the trees. After I've finished my section, I trim the branches and leaves around the trees. I have seven children and the older three help me with this job before they go to the farm school in the afternoon.

By 11 a.m. the latex has dripped from the trees into the small cups that hang on their trunks. I pour the liquid, which has already begun to thicken into a gluey mass, into a pail and take it to the roadside to be collected.

The latex is delivered to the farm's small factory. There it is put through a boiling process to harden it. The less water there is in the rubber, the better the quality will be. Afterward, it is washed, granulated,

Jandira and her family live in one of these houses provided for them by Pirelli.

14

dried and packaged for delivery to the four Pirelli tire factories located in the south of Brazil.

The farm is quite small and produces about 2 million kg (4.4 million lb) of rubber per year. The farm is also used for research to find ways of making the trees produce more rubber. A cloning process is used to help the *seringueiras* grow bigger and thicker at a faster rate than normal. Smaller trees are cloned by implanting a part from one of the stronger trees. If this implant takes well, and the trees are not attacked by disease, such as South American leaf blind, they will grow rapidly. The same result cannot be obtained simply by planting seeds.

At the turn of the nineteenth century, Brazil was the world's major producer of natural rubber and Manaus was called the rubber capital of the world. Over the years, tons of rubber have passed through the port of Belem, and because there was so much trade the British built a beautiful market-place called "Ver-O-Peso" (See-the-Weight). It is still a bustling place

Jandira collects the latex from a rubber tree prior to its delivery to the factory.

where people arrive in their boats and canoes at 6 a.m. to buy and sell goods.

Since we came to live on the farm five years ago, we haven't been into the city much. Pirelli provides us with cheap housing in one of the five villas on the farm. Apart from a nursery and a school, the town also has a church, medical services and a social club which holds Christmas parties and other activities during the year. The men have formed their own soccer team. On weekends, games are played at the farm against other local teams.

To encourage us to use our land profitably, each family is entitled to a small plot where they can plant their own vegetables. Our garden has corn, beans and *mandioca* (cassava root). Lots of good things are provided for us here. We have opportunities to improve our lives. But what I value most is the education my children receive here. I hope that Pirelli never decides to close our farm.

"We catch cavala, arabaiana, sirigado and even shark"

Fishing from *jangadas* (sailing boats) has been the livelihood of Mario Soares and his family for several generations. He has fifty years of experience behind him, and in the northeastern fishing village of Iguapé, in the state of Ceará, he is one of the most respected fishermen.

All along the northeast coast of Brazil, fishermen set out to sea every morning at the crack of dawn. My father was a fisherman and so are my sons. It's a tradition in Iguapé.

Many types of boat are used by Brazilian fishermen. In Ceará, we use *jangadas*, simple rafts with wooden hulls and strong canvas sails. They don't have outboard motors so we don't have to buy gasoline, which is expensive.

The *jangadas* which my father used were crudely made from tree trunks. Water seeped in between the logs which meant that you couldn't sleep on them. Some fishermen still use these primitive rafts. Our boats are more watertight and allow us to make overnight trips. My *jangada* is 7 meters (23 feet) long. Four or five fishermen can sleep in the small, narrow hull of the boat.

On a day trip, we spend twelve hours at sea. I get up at four in the morning and set out with three or four other fishermen. We sail till one o'clock in the afternoon and then drop anchor. We use a 3-kg (6.6-lb) lead anchor with 200 meters (660 feet) of nylon cord and a feather bobber which enables us to measure the depth of the sea.

At Iguapé's local market, Mario tries to get a good price for his fish.

This way we can tell what kind of fish we might catch.

When we are out just for the day, we don't sail out to where the big fish swim. So our daily catch will be smaller fish with strange names like pirauna, saparuna branca, marikita, biquada. Usually, I fish with a line and hook. Sometimes we use nets, but only when fishing for small fish.

I prefer the overnight trips. They're more interesting and take us farther out to sea where we catch the big fish such as cavala, arabaiana, sirigado, carapitanga and even shark.

It's possible to make a decent living from fishing. One sirigado weighing 18 kg (40 lb) brings the equivalent of U.S. $20. The sharks we catch have as much as 200 kg (440 lb) of meat. These fish are usually exported, but the majority of our catch is sold to small inland companies within the state of Ceará. We also sell our fish to local people.

In my fifty years of sailing and fishing, I have learned to love the sea and my home town of Iguapé, with its sandy white dunes and tall coconut palms. Iguapé lies on Brazil's northeast "Golden Coast" which runs for 3,500 kilometers (2,175 miles) along the Atlantic Ocean. It's a beautiful area with a tropical climate, so we never have any cold weather. The temperature all year round is about 33°C (91°F).

I love the sea, but sometimes it can be frightening. I remember dreadful rain and wind storms out at sea. But there's been a terrible drought in the northeast with no rain for the last five years. Many Cearenses – people born in the state of Ceará – have been forced to leave their homes in the dry interior because their crops and cattle have died. They have moved to live in or near Fortaleza, the

Mario's Jangada *puts to sea at the start of a fishing trip.*

coastal capital of the state.

The days that I don't go out to sea, I do woodwork. It's a hobby that also brings in extra money. My son helped me set up a workshop in our backyard where I build chairs, tables and benches for the *jangadas*. There's no furniture factory near Iguapé. I make things to order for local customers. It's a nice little business to have on the side.

"Rio nestles between sea and mountains"

Jorge Tavares operates the cable cars on Rio de Janeiro's famous Sugar Loaf Mountain. He ferries tourists up the 395 meters (1,303 feet) to the top of the mountain where they can gaze down on the natural beauties of Rio, the *Cidade Maravilhosa* (Marvelous City).

The cable cars that I operate are a great tourist attraction – and I can understand why! It's a unique experience to ride in a glass bubble-like car to the top of Sugar Loaf Mountain, and see Rio at your feet. To reach the summit, you have to take two cable cars. The first ride is up 220 meters (726 feet) to Urca Mountain. Each car can carry up to 72 passengers. The cable that the car rides on is 575 meters (1,897 feet) long and made of 151 steel bands strong enough to last thirty to forty years.

A beautiful view overlooking Rio de Janeiro.

At this halfway stop, you can see Guanabara Bay, part of the winding coast of Rio. As the local yacht club and marina are located there, the bay is always full of luxurious boats. On the other side of the mountain is the Praia Vermelho or Red Beach, a calm bay with no high waves which is especially good for swimming. The city's shoreline is indented with bays and coves, broken by beautiful beaches and dotted with islands and mountains. The city of Rio nestles between the sea and the mountains.

Urca Mountain has its own restaurant, a souvenir shop and an outdoor theater where musical shows are held. When I get time off during the day, I like to sit on the benches and gaze at the city below with the cool ocean breeze gently blowing on my face.

The second cable car goes up to Sugar Loaf Mountain itself. The cable extension between the two mountains is 750 meters (2,475 feet). At the top you have a breathtaking view over the beautiful, long curve of the Copacabana Beach, and, in the distance, Rio's Corcovado Mountain. There one of Rio's most famous landmarks, the statue of Christ, stands with his arms outstretched, watching over the city.

Our busiest months are January and February, when it's summer in Brazil, and July when Brazilians have their winter holidays. All together there are thirty-two operators who work the cars, sixteen on each day's shift. We work every other day from 8 a.m. to 10 p.m. and get a three-and-a-half hour rest period. On nights when there are shows, we sometimes work until 5 a.m. On Urca Mountain, rooms are provided for employees to take naps. This is very important because we work with machines that require our constant attention and we can't afford to get tired on the job.

Working at Sugar Loaf is a great job. When I began three years ago, I went through a training program to learn how to operate the equipment. I also had a course in how to deal with the public, which was really helpful. Now I attend English classes where I learn such useful phrases as "The door is closing," "Watch your step" and a couple of jokes in English.

The jokes come in handy to distract foreign tourists who are afraid of the cable car or heights. As soon as I tell them a joke in their language, they forget their fears. When I first began riding the cable cars, I was a little frightened too, but in time I got used to it. If there's a strong wind or a rainstorm, we close the cable cars down because the safety of the passengers is most important.

On my days off, I like to go fishing with my brother-in-law for crabs and shrimp in Guanabara Bay off Governor's Island. Rio's ultra-modern international airport is located on the island so when we're waiting to pull in the net, we watch the planes taking off and landing.

The cable car travels toward Urca Mountain on its way to the top of Sugar Loaf.

"I like the costumes, the music and the excitement"

Jésus Henrique is one of Brazil's most famous *carnavalescos* (carnival fanatics). His greatest love is designing costumes to wear in the big carnival parade held in Rio de Janeiro to mark the beginning of Lent. Many of his exotic costumes win awards and are sold all over the world.

Rio is famous for its *desfile* (carnival parade) that takes place on the Sunday before Ash Wednesday, marking the beginning of Lent. Its origins are linked to the Catholic religion. During Lent, Catholics are obliged to do penance and make sacrifices. Before they enter into the solemn forty-day period leading up to Easter, they hold parties and dance all night long. The Portuguese brought this tradition to Brazil. But it was the Brazilians themselves who mixed European and African customs to develop their own rollicking celebration.

The carnival has always fascinated me. I like the glittery costumes, the music and the excitement of it all.

I used to work in Rio as a tailor, but making men's boring suits wasn't my idea of designing. I had more fun creating fantasy costumes using feathers and sequins. I wore these extravagant costumes in the *desfile* and felt like a real movie star. That's how I became a *carnavalesco*.

My whole life revolves around the car-nival. The costumes for it can't be made in a few days. They take months and can cost the equivalent of U.S.$8,000 each.

From November until carnival time in February or March, we work around the clock making our costumes. The elaborate ones I make are worn by *destaques*, per-

Jésus Henrique tries on his exotic costume, ready for the carnival celebrations.

sons chosen by samba schools to wear the costumes and prominently placed in the parade lineup.

Samba schools began as local clubs where people gathered to play music and dance. Today they have grown into great institutions with directors, a staff of composers, dancers and musicians who are occupied with the carnival every day of the year. Although there are many schools, only the best fourteen are chosen to participate in the big parade. Beija-Flor is my school and our colors are blue and white. Other top schools include Mangueira, Portela and Salgueiro.

Besides being a wild and joyous occasion, the *desfile* is a serious competition. A jury appointed by the government judges the schools on their all-round performance. Each school has seventy-five minutes to parade the marked distance. If the timing is not right, they lose points. The purpose of each school's presentation

A lively and colorful scene during Rio's world famous carnival parade.

is to tell a story through dance, music and visual display.

The schools focus on a theme which is usually some aspect of Brazilian history or culture, like the Portuguese navigators who discovered Brazil or the Indians of the Amazon region. The theme is portrayed in their floats, costumes and song. Each school also has a percussion unit dressed according to their theme. These drum beaters provide a constant rhythm and pulsating undercurrent so the members of the school can keep the tempo.

The Brazilian carnival parade is a tough contest and a magnificent spectacle. It's a time when rich and poor get together, and forget their problems. Although it only happens once a year, carnival is my life.

"25 million sacks of coffee beans per year"

Renaldo Antonio Guias, 18, is a coffee planter in the state of Parana. He and his family live and work on a farm near Londrina, the city which is historically known as the world's coffee capital.

Brazil is one of the world's major coffee-producing countries. The agronomists from the Brazilian Institute of Coffee (IBC), who visit the farm to give us technical advice, told me that about 25 million sacks of coffee beans are produced in Brazil per year. From all the coffee I plant and pick, I believe them!

The northern part of the state of Parana, where I live, has forty-eight coffee plantations and all together about 520 million

Renaldo has to work hard all year round to maintain the coffee fields.

trees. North of Parana in the states of São Paulo and Minas Gerais, there are huge fields of coffee too. Because the soil in the southeast is very fertile, the region is the agricultural center of Brazil.

I have worked with coffee since I was five years old. We always worked for others until five years ago when we moved to a farm in Ibiporã, 38 kilometers (23 miles) south of Sertanópolis, our hometown. We're still not the owners of a farm, but we have a share in Doralice which entitles us to a house and a regular supply of food, plus pay for our work. I earn the equivalent of about U.S.$1.40 per day, and work six days a week. On the farm, we plant coffee to sell. Between the rows of coffee trees we grow rice, beans and other vegetables. We also have dairy cows here to provide fresh milk, and pigs and chickens that are raised and later slaughtered for food.

Working the coffee fields is never boring because our jobs change with the seasons. From May to October, the plump, round coffee cherries turn from green to red and are ready for picking. July is usually the month when the crop is best. Before picking, we clear the ground below the plants of broken branches and leaves. After we've picked the coffee cherries, they're laid out to dry in the open air and sun for fifteen days. Afterward, they go through machines that remove their husks. The cleaned beans are then shipped out to coffee companies. Big firms buy the beans, which are green in their natural state, and roast them to a dark brown. Later they're ground, packaged and sold in the supermarkets. When you think about it, there's a lot of work involved from the time the crop is planted until it becomes a cup of

A view of the farm where Renaldo and his family work as coffee planters.

coffee. When we're not picking, we cultivate new plants. It takes two years before they begin to produce coffee cherries. We also maintain the fields. When it's time to spray the trees with insecticide, the IBC men come around with equipment and teach us how to do it. Without their help many trees would die from disease or be attacked by insects.

The biggest danger is a frost. If temperatures fall below −4°C (24°F) crops can be destroyed. I can remember seasons when I had to wear a jacket and gloves, but normally the weather here is good for growing coffee, with average temperatures ranging between 14° and 28°C (56° to 82°F).

I'm the oldest in our family of eight children. My parents and one of my brothers are coffee planters too. The other kids help out sometimes while my little sister stays at home and plays. It can be quite noisy having such a big family, so on my day off I like to get away. I usually go into Ibiporã to meet friends in the public square. If I can afford it, I like to take my girlfriend to the movies.

"I eat meat for breakfast, lunch and dinner"

"Toco" Lopes Camara is one of Brazil's traditional *gauchos*, a cowboy of the southern grasslands, or pampas. He runs the Alvorada Estância in the southernmost state, Rio Grande do Sul, 15 kilometers (9 miles) east of the border of Argentina and north of Uruguay.

People born in Rio Grande do Sul, Brazil's southernmost state, are called *gauchos*. My family have been *gauchos* for generations. Real *gauchos*, like myself, work on ranches as cowboys. My father was a cowboy too. He came from Uruguay and married my mother, who's Brazilian. They settled in the frontier city of Uruguaiana where I was born.

Many years ago, before the South American continent was divided into countries like Argentina, Paraguay and Brazil, and before the land barons and their black slaves arrived to establish ranches, cattle breeders would move their herds from the interior to the coast. Along the way, they would rest and graze their cattle at *estâncias* (rest stops). By the time the herds reached the coast, they would be nice and fat, so at market the breeders would get a good price for them.

I'm the *capataz* (foreman) on the ranch. My job is to see that the cattle are taken care of. The immense grassy plains in Rio Grande do Sul and the cool climate are excellent for raising the state's 33 million head of cattle, sheep and pigs. On our 1,700-hectare (4,250-acre) farm, we have about 1,000 head of cattle, 1,500 sheep and 100 horses. The cattle are checked

After a day's work, the gauchos *relax outside the stables.*

24

At the end of a hard day's riding, "Toco" and his men water their horses.

regularly to make sure they're healthy. We vaccinate them four times a year. I also look after the horses. They usually work on the farm but sometimes the owner likes to enter a few of them in races for fun.

We have our own traditions and practices that are quite different from the Brazilians who live farther north or in big cities. We're famous for our *churrasco* (barbecue). We season the meat with salt and water. Then we cook it slowly on spits over an open fire. I eat meat for breakfast, lunch and dinner.

A habit which we adopted from the Guarani Indians, who used to live in the area, is to drink *chimarrão* all day long. It's a bitter herb tea. We put the green leaves in a *cuia* (gourd). Then we add hot water and sip it through a straw called a *bomba*. The real Indians used *bombas* made of bamboo. Ours are made of aluminium and have a little sieve at the base to prevent the leaves from going up the straw. We carry around our *cuias* and a thermos of hot water. The first thing I reach for in the morning is my *chimarrão*.

Even our clothes are traditional. The billowy trousers we use are called *bombachas*. They're full at the waist and narrow at the ankle so they fit into our knee-high leather boots. Our wide buckle belts have several pockets to carry a watch, money and a knife. We use a bandana around our necks and broad-brimmed hats. Wrapped around our waists and covering one leg is a piece of leather. This serves as an apron and also protects us if the cattle rub up against us.

Throughout the year, the state of Rio Grande do Sul holds several *rodeos*. They're my favorite pastime. Alvorado Estância enters about thirty men. I take part in lasso throwing and riding broncos. The competition is international, with many Argentinians and Uruguayans coming across the border for the events.

"Alcohol costs 40 per cent less than gasoline"

Sergio Luis Nogueira runs his family's 80-year-old farm and distillery where they grow sugarcane and produce alcohol to fuel Brazil's alcohol-powered cars. His firm, Usina Açucareira Ester S.A., was among the pioneers involved in developing the country's Proálcool energy saving program.

In 1973, the government discovered that Brazil had a serious energy shortage. It realized that if the country continued to import expensive oil from the Middle East, we'd always have financial difficulties. So the government began a Proálcool Program to develop ways of using alcohol from sugarcane as a fuel to replace oil.

After several years of work, Brazilian chemists and engineers have found a way to make the engine of a car run on alcohol. First they tried converting gasoline-driven car engines to alcohol and later, with more success, designed a full alcohol-powered car. (It takes one ton of sugarcane to make 70 liters (19 gallons) of alcohol.)

When the program began, people laughed and made jokes about it because everybody thought cars, trucks and tractors could only run on gasoline and that sugarcane can only be turned into sugar for use as a sweetener. Very few people believed that it could be a success. But it is, and today we produce 8 billion liters

(2 billion U.S. gallons) of alcohol. This is twelve times more than we produced ten years ago. Of our total production, 80 percent is used to fuel cars. It's no longer taken as a joke.

The greatest advantage is that alcohol costs about 40 percent less than gasoline. Last year, about 75 percent of the cars sold were economical alcohol-powered models. Over one million alcohol-powered cars have been produced in Brazil. Soon we expect to mass-produce alcohol-powered trucks and tractors.

My family has been in the sugar business since 1905. In the early years, we used to produce alcohol to make rum and sugar. Later we began selling it to chemical companies and in 1973 entered into fuel production. Brazil's sugarcane harvest is from May to November. At that time we cut the stalks in the field. Then we grind them to extract their juice. This liquid is cleaned of impurities and prepared in huge tanks. About 40 percent of it will become crystallized sugar. The rest will be fermented and eventually turned into alcohol.

Our factory is in the small town of Cosmópolis, about three hours drive from São Paulo. There are many sugarcane plantations in the interior of São Paulo state, and most of the country's alcohol fuel distilleries are located near them. About 235 of Brazil's 439 alcohol fuel projects are in this region.

Besides running the family business, I'm the President of the Association of Sugar and Alcohol Producers. Although this takes up a good deal of my time, it's very important to me. Our work is to unite the alcohol producers and to make sure Brazil's Proálcool Program continues to be a success.

Cosmópolis has a population of 23,000. Many of the city's residents work at Ester. We're a small community, almost a family. On weekends, I play soccer with the employees. Our company competes regularly with other local teams. I like to spend time getting to know my employees and the weekend soccer games are a good way of doing this.

At the Ester distillery, Sergio checks out the vats where the alcohol is produced.

Ester employees set out to work on the sugarcane plantation.

"I have created over 200 wall-paintings and sculptures"

Francisco Brennand is a sculptor and painter who rebuilt his family's abandoned ceramic factory in Recife. He turned it into one of Brazil's major art projects reflecting the Pre-Columbian culture and the Mediterranean influence brought over by the Portuguese.

I became interested in painting when I was thirteen years old. My father owned a small ceramic and tile factory called Cerâmica São João da Várzea on the outskirts of Recife in the northeastern state of Pernambuco. He invited artists from Europe to help him design the tiles. In the early 1900s, Europeans still had great influence on Brazil, so their opinions on tile designs were very important. I used to listen to them talk and was inspired to

In front of his rebuilt ceramics factory, Francisco shows his sculptures to visitors.

try painting for myself.

In 1949, I went to Paris to study art and to my surprise discovered that the Spanish artist, Picasso, one of the world's greatest painters, also worked with ceramics as an art form. I was so impressed that I thought I'd experiment with ceramics. When I returned to Brazil, I stopped painting and worked only with clay.

While I was abroad, my family had closed the factory in order to concentrate on our sugar mills. Since the sixteenth century, sugar has been an important commodity in the economy of Pernambuco. Even today it is one of Brazil's leading products.

The ceramic factory remained abandoned until 1971 when I decided to convert it into an experimental art center where I could display my sculptures and tiles. It took me twelve years of hard work to build, and it's still not finished.

When I thought up the project, I was influenced by both the Mediterranean and the Pre-Columbian cultures. The Mediterranean influence came to Brazil via the Portuguese settlers who also brought with them bits and pieces of the Arabic and African cultures. They were excellent craftsworkers when it came to ornamental tiles. The Pre-Columbian culture is found on Marajó Island in the northern state of Para. This Pre-Columbian civilization of Indians left behind some splendid ceramic vases and drawings.

To make ceramics, I use three types of clay – red, white and gray – which come from the states of Pernambuco and Piaui. My ceramics are very heavy and look old because I bake them several times in an extremely hot oven. I paint the clay with metals. Iron produces a red shade, copper a blue one and tin, a white one. During the baking process a chemical reaction

Francisco Brennand's wall designs are found on buildings throughout Recife.

occurs which brings out the beauty of the ceramic piece and gives it a natural shine.

Being an artist is very time consuming. I have created over 200 wall-paintings and sculptures which decorate buildings throughout Recife, the capital of Pernambuco and sixth largest city in Brazil. I used to hold exhibitions in art galleries, but today my own factory serves as a permanent showroom.

Sometimes my wife and I go into Recife. The coastal city is built on three rivers, each spanned by many bridges. Recife means reefs, and as the tide goes out rocks slowly appear on the city's beaches. We used to visit Recife more often but now it has grown into the major industrial center for the northeast region with all the hustle and bustle of a big city. My wife and I prefer the peace and quiet of our old nineteenth-century country house, surrounded by fields. There we raise cattle and horses and spend time with our five grandchildren.

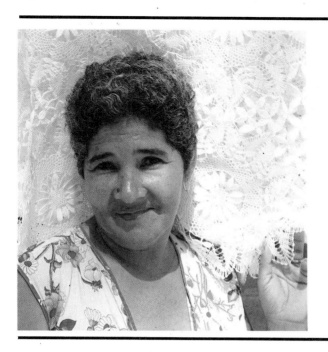

"A tablecloth takes two months to complete"

Carmelinda de Sousa is a *rendeira*, or lacemaker, who lives in the coastal village of Prainha, the major lacemaking center in the northeastern state of Ceará. Her beautiful handmade lace is a Brazilian folk art which the government is determined to preserve and promote.

When I was ten, my mother taught me to make lace. All the women in Prainha used to sit on the beaches twisting and braiding threads into lace while they waited for their fishermen husbands to return from the sea. Generation after generation of women learned the skill. Things haven't changed much today except that we now have the government's support.

Carmelinda and her partner use the bilros *to produce a huge lace bedspread.*

have seeds from the coconut tree attached at their ends, I guide the yarns, braiding and twisting them to make a piece of lace.

Depending on the design, I can use as many as fourteen *bilros*. It takes me about four days to make one round doily, 0.3 meters (1 foot) in diameter. A tablecloth needs close to forty of these doilies and takes two months or longer to complete. A bedspread takes twice as long. The smaller lace pieces I produce are used to decorate blouses and lingerie.

Since the government began supporting *artezanato* (folk art), Brazilians see the importance of our skilled crafts. This makes me happy because each piece of lace is a work of art. Each region of Brazil has its own distinct folk art. In the northeast area, there is a strong tradition of folk art. Besides lace work, there are wood carvings, embroidery, straw baskets, clay statues and leather goods. One has to understand that the Brazilian northeast is less modern and developed than the central and southern regions. Therefore, it has a lower standard of living. Outside the cities in the northeastern states, we lead very simple lives. There are few jobs going, so the crafts we can make at home and sell, help us to earn a living.

Prainha is a very quiet and simple village with a beautiful sandy beach. But besides our work, there's not much to do here. Once a year, in November, we have a procession of boats in honor of Our Lady of the *Navagadors*, one of our patron saints. We decorate the fishing boats with colorful banners and sail them down the coast. My husband is a fisherman and invites me to go along, but I'm afraid of the sea and would rather stay on shore and watch.

In years gone by, tourists who came to enjoy Prainha's lovely beach, used to knock at our doors asking if we had any lace to sell. But then two years ago, the former governor's wife, Luisa Tavares, founded a lace market in the public square of the village. Now we don't have to sell the lace from our homes. We take our work to the center and display our handmade lace items in the booths constructed by the government.

I think it's better this way because the market attracts more customers, so we can earn more. Our lacemaking is particularly popular with tourists and Brazilians from the more developed areas of the country, like São Paulo and Rio de Janeiro.

When my mother first taught me the craft of lacemaking, I found it difficult, unlike my two daughters, who picked it up very quickly. Eventually, with practice, I became quite an expert. I design my own patterns of little flowers or geometric shapes on paper. The pattern is pinned on to a big, fat pillow stuffed with banana leaves. Using sticks called *bilros* which

"I have collected over 7,000 insects"

Leocádio Gondim, 28, is a scientist at Brazil's National Institute for Research on Amazonia (INPA), based in Manaus. As part of his study of insects, he spent one year working in the Amazon rain forest collecting and studying them.

At least half of the ten to twelve million animal and plant species on this planet live within the Amazon jungle. Among the region's tropical foliage and waterways, there exist 1,800 species of birds, about 500 varieties of mammals, 1,500 types of fish and thousands of species of insects.

My speciality is insects. Ever since I was a boy living in Fortaleza in the state of Ceara, I was fascinated by insects. A colorful and pretty beetle called *joaninha* (ladybug) was my favorite. I used to capture and collect them. That early boyhood love explains why I chose to become an entomologist, which is a person who studies insects.

As I enjoy catching insects and studying how they live, I'm lucky to be working in the rich Amazon rain forest where about one-third of the world's million or so species of insects live. Because there's a shortage of entomologists in the world, a complete study of the Amazon's insects has yet to be done. We still have lots to learn, but our time is running out.

Some scientists say that in a few years' time, the forests and jungles of the Amazon region will no longer exist, because

Leocádio enjoys riding his bike to the INPA laboratory at the start of a day's work.

The leaves of these giant floating lilies can grow to more than 7 feet in diameter.

they are being so rapidly destroyed by men who are building roads and housing settlements with no thought of protecting the natural habitat. I am one of a group of about 250 scientists from many parts of the world who work together with Brazilians to research and study the fauna and flora of the Amazon.

A few years ago, when I was studying for an examination, I had to observe communities of insects inside the rain forest. I found an old abandoned farmhouse near a stream, about 40 kilometers (64 miles) from Manaus, and spent one week every month for a whole year working there. I gathered insects, including microscopic ones, from the rocks, tree trunks, fallen leaves, water and sand. Sometimes I had to dive into the streams with a mask and snorkel to find certain species.

One night in this lonely place in the dark jungle, there was a big storm with thunder and lightning. For the first time in my life, I was really scared. I felt totally powerless and began to understand why the Indians, who lived in the forest, feared these forces of nature and treated them like gods.

As a result of my work, I collected over 7,000 insects which I kept in small glass containers filled with alcohol to preserve them. Among these 7,000, I identified 218 different species. In the forest areas where I gathered insects, the caddis fly was most numerous. It's an insect that resembles a butterfly. In the areas cleared of trees, I found many kinds of mosquitoes.

I like being an entomologist because it puts me in close contact with nature and its insects, animals and plants. I hope that the Amazon region will not be destroyed, because it is a beautiful area that needs to be preserved.

"Most Brazilians are eager to learn English"

Alexandra Zunino is an 11-year-old schoolgirl who lives in Florianópolis, the capital of the state of Santa Catarina. She works hard in school and keeps busy with extracurricular activities such as piano lessons and ballet classes.

I go to school at the Colegio Coração do Jesus (Heart of Jesus College). It's a Catholic primary school. Our uniform is a white blouse, red skirt, white ankle socks and dark shoes. My school day begins at 7:45 a.m. in the morning and ends just before lunch time at 11:45 a.m. We have a twenty-minute break at 10 a.m. Of all my classes — which include geography, history, math, Portuguese, religion and gym — my favorites are science, art and English.

I really want to learn English. After I finish school, I take extra English lessons in the afternoon. My private classes have only about ten students compared to forty-three in my normal class. I like the smaller group because I get to speak more and the teacher has time to help us individually. We also use audio-visual aids. These films and records make the class more fun. Also the language school's library has a good selection of English books which are helpful. Most Brazilians are eager to learn English because it is spoken all over the

world, unlike Portuguese. My dream is to visit Disneyland in the United States where I can use the English I have learned.

My father speaks English. He's the chief pathologist at the Santa Luzia Laboratory in Florianópolis. He studied medicine in the U.S. As a pathologist, he studies the origins and development of disease. I find his work interesting and often visit the laboratory. I think that when I grow up, I'd like to be a doctor.

Apart from my studies, I also have ballet classes and piano lessons. I prefer ballet because we wear fun clothes like leotards, brightly colored leg-warmers and head-bands. First we do warm-up exercises. Then the teacher shows us new steps and jumps and we practice them to music. I like the jumps best.

Sometimes I get nervous and make mistakes, especially when I have to perform in front of an audience. We did two shows for parents at the school last year. Each ballet group created their own dance routine. Ours was called "A Journey

Ballet is one of Alexandra's favorite hobbies. Here she is at the bar exercise.

through Disneyland." When I was practicing alone in the teacher's room before going on, I did the steps perfectly but when I got on stage, I was so nervous that I made some mistakes.

We live in the coastal city of Florianópolis which is split in two by a bay of water. Half of the city is on the mainland and the other half on Santa Catarina Island. Our house is on the mainland, right on the beach. I like living there because of the water. My brother, two sisters and I spend a lot of time swimming or playing with our neighbors on the beach. Because the water in the bay is so calm, it's excellent for water sports, especially windsurfing and boating.

Alexandra stands outside her school dressed in her red-and-white uniform.

"I work sixteen-hour days"

José Carlos Pereira das Neves is a member of Brazil's military police force. When he's not on duty, he helps his wife run the family drugstore in Cordovil, a suburb of Rio de Janeiro, where they live.

Brazil's military police force is different from the civil police. We are trained to be both soldiers and policemen. Our job is to help protect people, but at the same time we're military reserves. So if there were a national crisis, like a war, we would be called on to fight. Fortunately, Brazil is a peaceful country and we have had no reason to go to war with our neighbors during this century.

I joined the military police, which everyone calls by the initials PM, in 1979 when I was twenty-three years old. I spent six months in a rigorous training pro

José Carlos chats to a fellow policeman outside the PM cabin near Ipanema Beach.

gram at the training center for enlisted men in Maracheal Hermes on the outskirts of Rio de Janeiro. We had to complete courses in marksmanship, police techniques, first aid, human relations and physical fitness. Our training was very strict, and the discipline harsh.

For the last three years, I've been working the "beach beat" in Rio. Blue and white PM cabins are located on corners throughout the city. These small cabins serve as mini-police headquarters. The one I work at is near the Ipanema Beach. If someone picks your pocket on the street or you lose your child on the crowded beach, you can come to us for help rather than going all the way to central headquarters or calling up on the phone. We are equipped with radios and we can summon help immediately.

Our motto, which is painted on the outsides of the cabins, says we are "faithful friends, brothers and comrades" to the people. Because we are badly needed, we work long hours. For three weeks, I work sixteen-hour days with an eight-hour break. During my rest period, I sleep, go to the movies or make a quick visit to my home in Cordovil. The fourth week of the month, I work an eight-hour shift every day.

Crime in Brazil's urban centers is a serious problem. To protect the citizens, PM units patrol areas on foot and in cars. The beach police ride in beach buggies, while white-and-blue Volkswagens with the military police emblem patrol other areas of the city.

We also have patrol units of three soldiers and one sergeant that are called *patamos*. They travel in trucks and are sent out to handle the more serious cases. Within the PM, there's also a unit called the "shock troop." These are the really

On weekends, José Carlos helps his wife run their family drugstore in Cordovil.

tough guys who are called up to control riots or large public gatherings, such as strikes, that could get out of hand.

My job can be as simple as giving directions to a tourist or as dangerous as chasing armed robbers. Once, three thieves tried to break into a house in the well-to-do residential area of Ipanema. The doorman came running to us for help. Immediately my group took off after them. It was risky because they had guns. Luckily, we caught the bandits without any shots being fired.

As a military policeman, I don't have much free time. When I go off duty, I go to work again! My wife owns the Leila Pharmacy in Cordovil. It used to be owned by my father, and when he died, she didn't want to close the traditional drugstore. So she worked hard to keep it open and is now the proud owner of the store. I help her whenever I get the chance.

"Brasília was carefully planned and designed"

Brasília, the capital of Brazil, was opened in 1960. This young and growing city needs schoolteachers like Graça Miziara to educate its first generation of citizens, who are the future of this new and promising city.

I've been teaching in Brasília, the nation's modern capital, for fifteen years. Building work on Brasília began in 1957 and continued at a frantic pace twenty-four hours a day, seven days a week until it was completed. The city was opened on April 21 1960 by President Juscelino Kubitschek whose dream it was to move the capital from the coastal city, Rio de Janeiro, to the interior state of Goiás. Twenty-four years later, Brasília already has a population of about 1,200,000. My family and I arrived when it was only a few years old. My father worked for the government in the state of Minas Gerais and was transferred to Brasília.

When I finished my studies at the University of Minas Gerais, I returned to Brasília and began teaching. For the last thirteen years I've been a teacher at the school, Colégio Nossa Senhora do Rosário. It's a Catholic school but you don't have to be a Catholic to go there and you aren't forced to attend classes on religion. The school was finished in 1959, so it's one of the oldest schools in Brasília. Today we have about 1,200 students, from age four to fourteen, and forty-seven teachers.

This is the Colégio Nossa Senhora do Rosário where Graça works as a teacher.

I teach math and science to eleven-year-olds. I really enjoy my job. I particularly like this age group because the students speak up for themselves but aren't too cheeky! The only problem I sometimes have is helping new students get used to living in such a modern city as Brasília. We still receive many new students whose families have moved to Brasília from the big overcrowded cities like Rio de Janeiro or São Paulo. At first, they have trouble making friends and feeling at home. Some people think it's an unfriendly city because it doesn't have roots yet, but I think Brasília is a pleasant and comfortable place to live.

The city was carefully planned and designed by two of Brazil's famous architects, Lúcio Costa and Oscar Niemeyer. They made sure that Brasília had lots of space. The city is laid out in the shape of an airplane with a body and two wings, one north and one south, with a main highway running through the two wings. The road has plenty of traffic circles and underpasses to help avoid traffic jams. Two artificial lakes have been made, one on each wing.

Most people live in *superquadras* (apartment blocks). The first ones built along the main highway are surrounded by trees and lawns to help cut down noise and air pollution. None has more than six floors. Each unit of four *superquadras* has its own elementary school, playground, stores and supermarket. As Brasília grows outward, beyond the two wings of the city, the area is still similarly divided into blocks so that it expands in an organised way.

My husband and I live in an apartment with our four-year-old son. Although I must admit it was unusual at first, we're used to Brasília and now wouldn't dream of leaving.

Graça meets her class to congratulate them on passing their exams.

"We spend a lot of time on the beach"

Brazil's vast northeast region consists of two fairly distinct regions: the *sertão* inland, and the coast. Marlene Araujo da Souza grew up in the *sertão* of Paraiba State and later moved to the coastal city of João Pessoa where she married and started a family.

I grew up in the *sertão*, which is the inland region of the northeast area. In the *sertão*, the land is dry, hard and strewn with rocks. Shrubs, cactus and thorn cover it

In a suburb of João Pessoa, Marlene stops to chat with neighbors.

and there's little vegetation. Cattle raising used to be a way of life but the region has been faced with several droughts over the last 100 years so many people have moved to live on the coast, or to Brasília and the southeast.

After I finished school, I left the *sertão* too. I came to João Pessoa to work as a

housekeeper for a family. Later, I met my husband, Carlos Antonio. We now have our own house and family. Carlos Antonio works as a waiter at the big, modern Hotel Tambau located on Tambau Beach. The hotel attracts many tourists from Brazil and other countries. It has helped to develop a tourist industry and create jobs. Although situated on the waterfront, it doesn't have its own private beach because by Brazilian law all beaches are public and to be enjoyed by everybody.

I often take our two children, Carla, who is two years old, and Jefferson, one year old, to Tambau Beach. The northeast coast has many beautiful beaches with fine white sand and blue-green waters. João Pessoa is the most easterly point in Brazil and has sun all the year round with average temperatures of 35°C (95°F). We spend a lot of time on the beach.

Besides outdoor activities, Carlos Antonio and I like to go to *forro* dances on weekends. After World War II, many Americans stayed in the northeast of Brazil and they used to hold dances which were open for all. The expression "for all" caught on. But the Brazilians couldn't pronounce the English phrase and it came out more like *forro* (fôhô). That's how they got their name. The music at these dances is played by a band of musicians using an accordion, triangle, tambourine and drum. *Forro*, with its special sound and skippy dance step, has become a tradition in the northeast.

We have other customs here that differ from the rest of Brazil. In our cooking, we use a lot of *mandioca* (cassava root). This root is ground into flour, called *farinha*, which we sprinkle over rice and beans or cook with butter in a frying pan to make *farofa*. Also the gum from the *mandioca* is used to make tapioca. We mix it with

Brazil's northeast coast has many beautiful beaches like this one.

grated coconut, form small patties and bake them on a griddle over a fire. Served with coffee, they make a delicious breakfast. We even use the *mandioca* to make sweet cakes called *pe-de-moleque*.

On the coast, fish is an important part of our diet and *peixadas*, fish and vegetables cooked in a fish soup, are popular. The most plentiful fruits in Paraiba are the *caju* which give us the cashew nut and pineapple.

Life in the northeast is simple but pleasant. My sister and my mother-in-law also live with my husband, the children and me. Even though our house has only three small rooms, we all manage to get along. To live as one big, happy family under one roof is very important to us Brazilians.

41

"The samba rhythm gets into our blood"

Pedro Marcos Ferreira Pottier, 27, is a musician with the samba group Estrela Negra ("The Black Star"). He plays the *agogô*, a unique Afro-Brazilian instrument made of steel cones. His musical tours take him to many cities in Brazil and abroad to Europe and Africa.

Brazilian samba has a long history. Basically it's a mixture of European folklore and African rhythms blended together over the last 100 years. It is especially popular in Rio de Janeiro where I live.

I grew up in Nilópolis, an area in Rio de Janeiro's north zone, which is the industrial working-class region. We *Cariocas* (natives of the city of Rio) really love samba music and dance. We grew up with it. The samba rhythm gets into our blood and becomes a very important part of life. When I was eight years old, I learned to dance the samba at the local youth club. Then, when I was a teenager, I began to play the instruments and dance in local samba shows, and I've never looked back.

There are seven musicians in our group, Estrela Negra, and each of us plays a different instrument. Jorge plays a huge, deep bass drum, called the *surdo*, which gives samba its backbone. The *pandeira* is a large tambourine, about the size of a frying pan, with metal, coin-like pieces around the edge; Fio plays it with his hand and often twirls it on one finger as he dances. Marcello plays an unusual instrument called the *reco-reco* – a metal tube with notched rods that are grated with a stick to create a constant rhythmic sound. The tambourine is smaller than the *pandeira*; Juvenil plays it with a stick rather than using his hand. Rubens plays the *cavaquinho* (ukulele), which adds harmony to the group. One of the most exceptional instruments is the *cuica* which Alcir plays. It is a friction drum resembling a small keg which is open on one side. There's a stick inside attached to the membrane, and when Alcir rubs it with a moist cloth squeaky rhythmic sounds come out. My instrument, the *agogô*, is made of two linked steel cones that are beaten with a rod. Its sound is similar to a bell with two different tones. I accompany the samba rhythm of the other instruments, always keeping in time with them.

Besides our regular shows in Rio, we often make musical tours throughout

During the carnival, Pedro and Estrela Negra perform the samba on the streets of Rio.

Brazil, playing in all the major cities. On our trips abroad to Europe and Africa, I'm always surprised how foreigners pick up the samba beat and their feet start to move. The samba step itself isn't difficult to learn, but to dance it well, you have to feel it in your heart. The time of the year when samba really explodes is carnival. On the four days and nights before Ash Wednesday, Estrela Negra performs in the street parade where samba is at its best.

As a musician most of my shows are at night or on weekends. During the day I work at a small accounting firm that my cousin, William, and I started two years ago in Nilópolis. We handle accounts for local stores and garages. But to tell you the truth, I prefer being a musician: it's more fun.

Pedro playing the agogô *with the samba group Estrela Negra.*

"We call on the gods and spirits of Africa"

Daldina da Conceição de Assis is a *Mãe de Santo*, a spiritual priestess of the ancient gods of Africa. She and her followers practice *Candomblé*, the mystical Afro-Brazilian religion brought to Brazil by their African ancestors. Her cult is particularly strong in the northeastern state of Bahia.

Most people find it difficult to understand my religion. They think it's some kind of voodoo brought from Africa to Brazil as far back as the sixteenth century, but that isn't correct. When they were brought here as slaves, my ancestors practiced a religion similar to the one they had in Africa. They would chant, beat drums and ask the gods to descend to Earth. However, their white masters and the Catholic missionaries in Brazil forced Christianity upon them. In order to avoid punishment, the slaves had to practice their religion secretly, and so they disguised their gods by giving each one of them a name of a Catholic saint.

Gradually, the pure African religion became mixed with Christianity. It also borrowed certain powers from the Indians who have strong mystic beliefs and worship the forces of nature too. As time went by, our religion changed according to the new needs of our people in Brazil. Among the various cults that exist today in Brazil, *Candomblé* comes closest to maintaining its pure African form. The others, called *Macumba*, *Umbanda* and *Quimbanda*, are similar but they have been adapted to modern times. In the state of Bahia, where

Paintings of the gods decorate the walls of the Candomblé *temple in Salvador.*

44

the black population is largest, there are at least 1,200 *Candomblé* centers.

My father came from Africa and set up a *terreiro* (temple), where he practiced *Candomblé*. He was a *Pai de Santo* – father of the gods. Because of his influence, I became an active participant in *Candomblé* and, after fulfilling the necessary obligations, became a *Mãe de Santo*. I practice my religion at a *terreiro* run by a *Pai de Santo*. He is the most important person and oversees the ceremonies.

According to our religion, each person is under the protection of an *orixa* or god. Ogum, who is represented as Saint Anthony, is one of my gods and acts as a father symbol. Yansã, who is Saint Barbara, is the goddess who assumes the role of mother to me. Some of our other gods are Yemanjá (the Blessed Virgin Mary), Oxalá (Jesus Christ), Omolú (Saint Lazarus), and Exu, who is the devil.

When we hold a ceremony, we call on the gods and spirits of Africa to descend into the bodies of their children. We beat drums, chant, dance and meditate as our ancestors did so that the gods will come. Certain privileged members called *Filho de Santo* (son of the gods) are mediums who are prepared, according to the rules of our religion, to receive the gods. During a ceremony, a *Filho de Santo* will go into a trance as a god takes possession of his body. As a *Mãe de Santo*, I must watch over the mediums until the god leaves, calm the god if he becomes too violent and see that he receives his favorite food. Each god has his own personality. For example, Ogum likes to eat beans, yams and the bull's liver, heart and lungs. He is the divine blacksmith and the war god. He dwells in the forest, and when he dances he triumphantly waves a sword and has a ferocious look on his face.

During the ceremony, I wear white clothes in honor of Oxalá. My beaded necklace is blue because that's the color of my *orixa*, Ogum. I wear a turban before the gods descend. Once they are amongst us, I exchange it for a festive headdress symbolic of the *orixa* whose day we are commemorating.

I've been a *Mãe de Santo* for fourteen years. My religion is very important to me: it's a source of personal strength through union with natural forces and psychic energies. But, besides being a *Mãe*, I'm an ordinary Brazilian. I'm married and have one daughter. During the day I work as a cook, and when I have free time, I like to dance and drink beer.

45

"I dress like the slaves in colonial times"

Eulina Rosa is one of the many traditional *Baiana* figures found on the streets and squares of Salvador, in the state of Bahia. For thirty years, she has been cooking and selling delicious salty snacks and homemade desserts to hungry Brazilians.

Since I was a young girl, I've enjoyed cooking the Afro-Brazilian specialities that my mother taught me to make. Every weekend, I load up the family van and go to the Amarelinho Square near the beach to sell my snacks and sweets. I have many customers who return to my *tabuleiro*, the tray I use for displaying my food. They say I make the best *acarajé* in Salvador.

The *acarajé* is one of the most popular snacks. It's hard work to prepare it, using old-fashioned methods, but I'm used to it, so it's easy for me. The batter is made of dried beans called *fradinho*. I soak them overnight and then remove their outer skins. As I mash them into a smooth paste, I add water, onions, dried shrimp and seasoning. When the batter is ready, I drop it by spoonfuls into hot *dendê* oil, taken from the African palm tree that grows in Brazil.

As the *acarajés* fry, they puff up like big, plump dumplings. This same dough can be cooked by wrapping it in banana leaves or corn husks and steaming it. When prepared this way, we call it *abará* and serve it cold. Both the *acarajé* and the *abará* can be served with a hot pepper sauce and a mixture of dried shrimp and *dendê* oil.

The Lacerda Elevator connects the upper and lower parts of the city of Salvador.

Vatapá and *moqueca* are two other popular Bahian dishes that are served throughout Brazil. They're both made with fish and heavily laced with *dendê* oil.

I also prepare desserts to sell. Many customers buy my *cocadas* which are very sweet and made of freshly grated coconut mixed with white or brown sugar. Sometimes I make *cuscuz*, a dessert which originated in Arabia and was brought to Brazil by the Africans. It is made of tapioca, sugar and coconut. Brazilians love sweet food!

Salvador was the first capital of Brazil. Many slaves were brought from Africa to help build it. When they crossed the Atlantic Ocean, they brought with them their traditional way of cooking, so the cookery of the Bahia region has an interesting history. Many Brazilians are descended from those slaves, and 60 percent of people who live in Salvador today are black.

When I go to work, I dress as the slaves did in colonial times when they worked in the kitchens of the big sugar plantations. I wear either a white or gaily-colored full skirt and petticoat with a white, lace-trimmed blouse and always a turban on my head. Each color of my beaded necklaces represents a saint from my Afro-Brazilian religion, *Candomblé*. I wear these for protection. My religion is very important to me. Almost everyone who enters the *Candomblé* religion has to perform a service for the public. I chose to make and sell food as mine.

I was born in Salvador and have never lived anywhere else in all my sixty-three years. Salvador is divided into an upper and lower city. The two cities are connected by the Lacerda Elevator which bridges the 65-meters (250-foot) distance. A popular place to sell Bahian food is in the lower city near "Mercado Modelo," which is the market on All Saints' Bay. This area is always bustling with people hungry to eat our specialities.

Eulina prepares the acarajé *and other Bahian foods at her* tabuleiro.

"We heard that Brazil was a land of opportunity"

Shizuko Takahashi is a Japanese immigrant who came to Brazil twenty-five years ago. She and her husband, Takeshi, are gardeners. They sell their plants at the Oriental Fair held in the district of Liberdade, the traditional stronghold of the Japanese, Chinese and Korean communities in São Paulo.

My husband and I came to Brazil after World War II, which was fought from 1939 to 1945. It was very difficult to make a living in Japan and when we heard that Brazil was a land of opportunity, we decided to move. We left our home in Hokkaido in the cold north of Japan for the warm weather of southeastern Brazil.

We settled in the town of Atibaia about 66 kilometers (40 miles) from the big industrial city of São Paulo. Atibaia is famous for growing fruit and flowers. As we are experienced gardeners, we were able to find work quite easily.

It wasn't difficult to get used to Brazil, apart from learning the language. I found Portuguese was very hard to learn, especially because we lived among Japanese people who make up 20 percent of Atibaia's population.

The cold weather in Japan meant we could only plant for six months in each year, but here we can work all year round. In Atibaia, we have a garden full of plants, pine trees and *bonsai*, a traditional Japanese art of growing dwarf trees. On Sundays, we load up our van with plants and go to the Oriental Fair held in the district called Liberdade in the center of São Paulo. We set up a stall on the main street and sell our plants. Liberdade is full of people like ourselves from the Far East, including Chinese and Koreans.

Selling plants is a good business so long as we do not get caught in a downpour! Last year ferns were very popular. This year we sell more climbing-type plants, called *trepadeiras* in Portuguese. On a good day, we earn the equivalent of U.S.$150–U.S.$200.

My husband is one of the few gardeners at the fair who practice *bonsai*. By controlling the pruning and fertilization of trees, they come to look like small versions of big, ancient trees. We only have a few of these trees for sale. They are expensive and cost about U.S.$500. Besides gardening, I work during the week at the Ceasa market-place in São Paulo, selling fruit and vegetables.

Every Sunday, the Oriental Fair becomes the main attraction in Liberdade.

When my husband and I were settled in Brazil, we started a family. We now have five children. The oldest daughter is a dentist, the second-oldest girl won a scholarship to study in Tokyo in Japan and our two younger daughters and son are students in Brazil.

I like my life here. Brazilians are good people and we are seldom made to feel like strangers. The Japanese living in Brazil make up the largest community of Japanese outside Japan. There are 180,000 Japanese in Brazil, with 125,000 of us living in the state of São Paulo. Even after visiting Japan two years ago, and seeing how beautiful and modern it is, I don't want to return there to live. Brazil is my home.

The Takahashi stall at the Oriental Fair in Liberdade is full of plants.

"The largest Catholic population in the world"

Padre Jaime Hilgeman is an American Maryknoll missionary priest who came to Brazil to work with the poor. He lives in Jardim Veronia, which is a community run by Roman Catholic missionaries in the poverty-ridden outskirts of Brazil's largest city, São Paulo.

When I was a boy, I used to dream of traveling to Brazil and paddling a canoe up the Amazon River. My dreams changed when I became a missionary. I wanted to be able to work with the poor people in Latin America. For ten years I worked in Mexico before moving to Brazil in 1978.

I chose Brazil because Maryknoll missionaries were already doing exciting work there and also I wanted to learn a new language. Brazilians speak Portuguese whereas all the other Latin Ameri-

A view of the favela of Jardim Veronia shows how closely packed the houses are.

can countries speak Spanish.

I am a Roman Catholic priest and Brazil has the largest Catholic population in the world. Many years ago, priests came to Brazil after the Portuguese conquest and converted the local Indians to Catholicism. Today, the vast majority of a total population of 120 million people are baptized Catholics. We no longer have to convert people to Catholicism, so we are more concerned with improving the social conditions of the poor.

When I arrived in Brazil, I spent four months in Rio de Janeiro learning Portuguese. After that, I visited the slum districts of São Paulo, which is the biggest city in Brazil. It looks like a rich and prosperous city, but there is great poverty in many areas. São Paulo reflects the great contrast between rich and poor which is such a problem in modern Brazil.

I particularly liked one of our communities in São Paulo called Jardim Veronia, which is a suburb of Ermelino Matarazzo. I rented a simple three-room stucco house close to the *favela* (shanty town) that comes within the boundary of our community. For three years I've been sharing the house with Lucas, a twenty-year-old Brazilian friend.

In Jardim Veronia, I spend my days working with needy people to build a small Christian community which the Maryknolls call a "base" community. By living with the poor, I can understand their problems better and work toward solving them. The community needs paved streets, running water, regular waste disposal, schools, and medical services to fight such diseases as polio which still afflict Brazilian children.

Most of the neighbors work at the nearby glass and chemical factories. In some plants, working conditions are bad and wages low, the equivalent of about U.S.$200 per month. In the evenings, we hold neighborhood meetings at the homes of the workers to discuss what we can do to improve the working situation. We encourage the people to get involved in the development of their country. Very slowly, small improvements are being made.

I work with three other priests and seven nuns in an area which houses 170,000 Catholics. Four priests for all these people are not enough – like the rest of Brazil, we need many more priests. Brazil has only 12,000 priests to serve some 98 million baptized Catholics. We divide up our area so that each community has a priest to say Mass at least twice a month. When I say Mass in church, I use the traditional vestments of a priest. But when I'm working with the people in the *favela*, I'm one of them and dress like everyone else.

Padre Jaime chats to youngsters in the favela *where he lives and works.*

"We are trying to establish a democracy"

As a Federal Congressman, Jorge Vargas divides his work time between the country's capital, Brasília, and the state of Minas Gerais where he was born and whose people he now represents in Congress.

My father was an important influence in my life. He served as a town Mayor in Paracatu where I was born, and eventually a Congressman in our state, Minas Gerais. It was because of him that I became interested in politics and pursued a career in government.

I grew up in the inland state of Minas Gerais in the southeast region of Brazil. Together with its neighboring states, Rio de Janeiro and São Paulo, the three make up what's known as the "economic triangle." It is the richest and most densely populated area of Brazil. I was brought up in the small city of Paracatu in the northern part of the state. The area around Paracatu is mostly agricultural. There are lots of farms that produce coffee, soybeans and corn and some that raise cattle. The state is also rich in minerals so it is called the "mining state."

In 1962, when I became a State Congressman, I felt there was a need for more industry in the region and set out to develop it into a bigger industrial center. Today, we produce metals, ceramics and even have a few breweries. We contribute

Bruno Giorgi's sculpture "The Two Warriors" overlooks Brasília's Three Powers Square.

to what is considered the largest concentration of economic and industrial activity in Latin America.

In 1970, I became a Federal Congressman, which meant that I had to live in Brasília, the capital. At that time, Brasília was only ten years old. When my wife and our eight children moved to Brasília, we found it a bit strange. Brasília was so modern and friendless compared with our familiar home state of Minas Gerais. The children got used to the differences more quickly than my wife and I, but now, after fourteen years of life in Brasília, I have learned to appreciate the best of both the capital and Minas Gerais.

We are trying to establish a democracy with direct elections for government officials and the President. We hope that the constitution will develop to meet the needs of modern Brazilian society.

The structure of Brazil's present-day government and constitution is similar to that of the United States. We have a President, who, with the help of his Ministers of State, is in charge of running the country; the Supreme Court, where important law cases are dealt with; and the National Congress with its House of Representatives and Federal Senate, who are the people who make the laws. You'll find these government agencies within the Three Powers Square in Brasília.

Although I'm a politician, I am also a lawyer, as well as owning a cattle farm in Minas Gerais. When I'm not working, my favorite pastime is flying my small airplane and admiring Brazil's beautiful countryside.

A row of important government buildings in Brazil's capital, Brasília.

"The fifth largest country in the world"

Captain Drausio Leal is a pilot with Brazil's major internal airline, VASP (Viacao Aerea São Paulo). He is based in Rio de Janeiro, but spends most of his free time at his farm in Resende, 160 kilometers (100 miles) from Rio.

Brazil is the biggest of all South American countries and the fifth largest country in the world. It covers an area of 8,500,000 square kilometers (3,300,000 square miles). Geographically, we have so many different regions that when I fly from the great plains in the south to the tropical beaches in the northeast or the jungles bordering the Amazon River, I almost feel as if I have entered another country.

The distances within Brazil are so great that most of my flights have several stops. This is a typical flight which takes 4 hours. I leave Rio de Janeiro flying south to the

Passengers embark on a VASP flight at João Pessoa's airport.

industrial center of São Paulo. Then I make a stop in Campinas, 96 kilometers (50 miles) from São Paulo. I continue northward to Goiânia, the capital of the inland state of Goiás, and complete the journey in Brasília, the country's capital which is a federal district located within the state of Goiás.

I grew up near an air force base in São Paulo and loved to watch planes landing and taking off. When I was sixteen, I decided to study aviation and enrolled in a beginner's pilot course with hopes of eventually becoming a professional pilot. I was one of the lucky few to succeed. After a few years as copilot with a small airline, I was promoted to captain at the age of twenty-six.

Some of my most exciting trips with the airline were bringing workers into the dense Amazon jungle during the 1960s. I flew a plane called the Catalina, known by the Americans as "the old flying boat" because it could land on water.

During my trips between the cities of Belem in Brazil and Iquitos in Peru, I landed on the Negro River, one of the major tributaries of the Amazon River. I met Indians and foreign missionary priests who lived in jungle villages. Once I was invited by the Indians to go night fishing with them. Holding lighted torches over areas of the Negro River where fish were abundant, the Indians could see the fish underwater and would quickly spear them. It was a very interesting experience.

Today, my flights are less adventurous. I fly up to 100 hours per month for VASP. The airline has about twenty-five Boeing 737s, four Boeing 727–200s and two modern "Air Buses." Brazil's aviation system has improved tremendously over the last twenty years. Sophisticated radar has made flying safer and easier than when I

Captain Drausio relaxes at his farm in Resende with his dog, Biron.

first began to fly, especially in bad weather.

I enjoy being a pilot. I like the sensation of flying and bringing a plane down smoothly. I also like the responsibility I have as captain for planning the trip and making sure the crew and passengers are happy and safe.

Besides being a professional pilot, I also own a small farm in Resende. I like to spend every free moment at my farm. I raise dairy cows and plant crops such as sugarcane, carrots and lettuce. When I stop flying in a few years' time, I plan to retire to my farm, drink lots of fresh milk and never get up for another early morning flight!

"I often have to interview foreign diplomats"

Flavio de Almeida Salles is a journalist on one of Brazil's major newspapers, *Folha de São Paulo*. Based in Brasília he is in charge of covering foreign news. Besides interviewing diplomats visiting the capital, he also accompanies officials from the Brazilian Foreign Ministry on trips abroad.

I grew up in Penapolis, a small town in the state of São Paulo, where I worked for a short time on the local newspaper. I didn't intend to be a journalist. I was studying to be a lawyer at the law school in São Paulo but I found that I never had enough money so I decided to get a part-time job. The *Folha de São Paulo* was look-ing for journalists and asked me to go for an interview.

While I was waiting to be interviewed, I watched reporters rushing around, tele-

When not at work, Flavio relaxes by his swimming pool with his two children.

phones ringing, typewriters banging and photographers coming and going. I liked the sense of urgency and decided that journalism was the job for me. I passed the tests and was hired to work at the São Paulo office.

When I was just beginning my career as a journalist in 1964, the military took over the country. Brazil was faced with serious economic problems like inflation, high prices, scarcity of food and a lack of houses for the growing population. There had been disagreement among the politicians about how to solve these problems, and the military decided to take matters into their own hands. The newspapers needed more journalists in Brasília to report on the changing scene. I volunteered and was sent to the capital.

My first assignment was to write news about the Planalto Palace which is where the President conducts business. Later, I was assigned to the National Congress where I reported on Brazilian politics and the major decisions that the new government was making. In 1969, the government closed Congress and I was transferred to the international area. Eventually I was put in charge of foreign affairs coverage.

In Brasília, like any capital city, we receive international diplomats every day as well as ambassadors from countries with whom we have good working relations. I have to go to Brasília's international airport to interview foreign diplomats as they arrive and sometimes I attend press conferences at the embassies.

The most rewarding experience I have had as a journalist was to coordinate all the reporting of the 1980 visit of Pope John Paul II. Since Brazil has the largest Roman Catholic population in the world, religion strongly influences the lives of

Whenever Flavio gets a chance, he likes to show off his skill as a cook.

the people and so the Pope's visit was very important to us.

My job also involves accompanying official Brazilian missions abroad. One of the most interesting trips was to Africa. For several years, Brazil has been developing trade relations with African countries. The Brazilian subcontinent juts out into the South Atlantic, providing the closest point of physical contact between the Western Hemisphere and Africa. Also, African blood flows in the veins of a majority of Brazilians, so geographically and historically we are close to Africa.

Although I enjoy being a journalist, I felt it was important to complete my law studies. Today I work as both a lawyer and journalist and also teach classes on civil law at the Brasília Law School. With such a hectic schedule, I need to relax on weekends. I like to spend them at home with my wife and our two children. You'll find me either in the kitchen cooking my favorite meal or lazing by the swimming pool.

57

Facts

Capital city: Brasília.

Principal language: Portuguese.

Currency: Cruzeiro. Due to a high rate of inflation in Brazil the rate of exchange alters rapidly. Cruzeiro 1,400 = U.S.$1 (May 1984).

Religion: Roman Catholicism is the established religion. Brazil has the largest Roman Catholic population in the world. There are also Protestants, Jewish Spiritualists and those who adhere to *Candomblé*, the Afro-Brazilian religion.

Population: 119.0 million (1983). Brazil has the seventh largest population in the world. The density of population varies greatly. About 60% live in the south and southeast, which together comprise less than 18% of the total land area.

Climate: There are five climatic regions in Brazil: equatorial (warm and humid), semiarid (warm and dry), tropical (warm with a dry season), altitude tropical (mild throughout the year) and subtropical (warm summer, cool winter). Annual temperatures range from 28°C (82°F) in the semiarid northeast to 11°C (52°F) in the temperate south.

Government: Brazil is a republic. There is no royal family and the country is governed by a President with the help of his Ministers of State. They are assisted by the National Congress which has two "houses," the Senate and the Chamber of Deputies. Each of the twenty-three states within Brazil elects three senators and a number of deputies, corresponding to the population within each individual state. The states have a measure of independence from the central government which is based in the capital in Brasília. Each state has an elected Governor and an elected Assembly (Parliament).

Housing: About two-thirds of all Brazilians now live in urban areas, an explosive growth of more than 550% in the last 40 years. This rapid expansion has brought about serious housing problems, and most major cities have shanty towns on their outskirts. Various measures have been introduced to alleviate the problem but have met with only mixed success.

Education: Education in Brazil is on three levels: first level (elementary schools) for children from 7 to 14; second level (secondary schools) from 14 to 17/18; higher education at universities and colleges. About 90% of elementary schools are run by the state, but at the secondary level, over 50% of the schools are privately owned. 45 of the 65 universities are state-run. Many Brazilians are still illiterate (unable to read or write). The Brazilian Literacy Movement (MOBRAL) has succeeded in reducing the illiteracy rate from 34% to 21.8%.

Military service: This is compulsory. Every male must enlist at the age of 21 for one year's service.

Agriculture: One-third of the total workforce is employed in agriculture. Brazil is the world's largest producer and exporter of coffee and is recovering from the disastrous frost that ruined the crop of 1975. Brazil is also the world's largest producer of sugarcane. Other crops are wheat, tobacco, soybeans, rice, peanuts and various fruits. Brazil is one of the leading livestock producers in the world.

Industry: Brazil is the leading industrial nation in Latin America, and the car, ship and aircraft building industries are steadily growing. Mining for nonferrous metals is also on the increase. The third National Development Plan (1980–85) has led to growth in industrial output.

The Media: All major cities have their own newspapers. Five newspapers are distributed nationally. There are over 1,000 radio stations throughout Brazil, of which Radio Nacional is the official broadcasting station. Brazil has 6 television networks to serve 70 million viewers. Globo (with 70% of the "ratings") and Bardeirartes are the major national television networks.

The author and the publishers are indebted to VASP Airlines for their assistance towards the author's travel arrangements. All the photographs were taken by the author with the exception of the main cover picture, which is supplied by Marion and Tony Morrison, South American Pictures.

Glossary

agronomist A person who studies agricultural economics.

ambassador An important person, sent to a foreign nation to represent his or her own country.

cacao tree A tree that bears the seeds from which cocoa and chocolate are made.

ceramics The art of producing objects made from clay.

cult A type of religion, or a popular "craze."

democracy A type of government whose members have been voted for by the people.

distillery A factory where alcohol is made.

drought A long period without rain.

fauna The animal life of a region.

flora The plant life of a region.

gourd The dried fruit of a large plant, hollowed out and used to hold liquid.

inflation When prices increase more rapidly than wages.

meditate To think deeply about a subject.

medium A person through whom spirits of the dead are said to speak.

peddler A person who travels from place to place selling goods.

penance An act performed to show sorrow for wrong deeds.

reservation An area of land set aside for the use of native Indians.

rodeo A show of horse riding skills by cowboys.

silt A deposit of fine sediment in water, particularly in river tributaries.

species A group of similar animals or plants.

ukelele A small guitar-like instrument with four strings.

vaccination The injection of a viral substance into the blood for protection against disease.

voodoo A religion which involves witchcraft and communication with the dead.

Index

!F